THE CORNISH WORLD
OF
DAPHNE du MAURIER

BOSSINEY BOOKS

First published in 1995
by Bossiney Books, St Teath, Bodmin, Cornwall.

Typeset and printed
by Penwell Ltd, Callington, Cornwall.

© Curtis Brown, James Mildren, Michael Williams, Rebecca Pickford,
  Felicity Young, Sarah Foot, Jane Talbot-Smith, Douglas Williams

Extracts from Daphne du Maurier's work reproduced with permission of
Curtis Brown Ltd, London on behalf of the Chichester Partnership
Rebecca © 1938 by Daphne du Maurier Browning
Frenchman's Creek © 1941 by Daphne du Maurier
The Rebecca Notebook © 1981 Daphne du Maurier

ISBN 1 899383 02 6

ACKNOWLEDGEMENTS

Front cover: Roy Westlake
Modern photographs: Ray Bishop
Front cover design: Maggie Ginger

FERRYSIDE, formerly the residence of Miss Angela du Maurier and *now the home of Christian Browning and his family. Originally known as 'Swiss Cottage', the du Mauriers first rented the property and later bought it. The young Daphne wrote her very first novel* **The Loving Spirit** *at Ferryside. In the foreground is the Bodinnick-Fowey ferry.*

JAMES MILDREN, *who lives at Morice Town, Devonport, is one of the most respected journalists in the Westcountry today. Formerly on the staff of the* **Western Morning News**, *he retired from full-time journalism in 1988, and now works as a freelance writer and broadcaster.*

His **Castles of Devon**, *published by Bossiney in 1987, remains in print. In it, in the company of his sons, Julian and Stephen, he tours Castle Drogo, Lydford, Dartmouth, Watermouth and others.*

More recently he contributed **100 Years of the Evening Herald** *to the Bossiney list. As he says 'some century, some news!' Words and wonderful old photographs show how and why the* **Herald** *has become such 'a trusted and reliable family friend.'*

AN ENCHANTED PERSPECTIVE

by James Mildren

WORDS and books can be paradoxical memorials. Was Daphne du Maurier like the Rebecca (1938) of her most famous novel, as many of her readers believe? Or does she reveal herself, as she suggests, in a lesser-known work, *The Parasites* (1949)? Certainly, her principal characters were the product of her own turbulent, and at times, tormented, inner tensions. But there are other facets which cannot be ignored. She was, undoubtedly, greatly influenced and inspired by the countryside she knew best, and adored most – Cornwall's.

She first visited it as a small child: it failed to make much of an impression then. But when she came again, almost reluctantly, in 1926, she was enchanted. She had already begun to write short stories. Stories with atmosphere. Stories about Brittany, where she had stayed briefly, soaking up the feel of the place, absorbing its essential Frenchness with which she was, through ancestry, able to relate instantly. At the age of 19, she undoubtedly would have preferred to spend more time in France. Had it been the 1990s, with all its ease of travel, and not the 1920s, it is possible that Daphne du Maurier might have made her home in France.

Writing is a solitary business, but not all writers are solitary people. Daphne du Maurier was one of Nature's recluses. She was blessed with a vivid imagination. She had the talent and good sense, however, to control it. In her work, the touch of the sinister, the supernatural even, is never allowed to degenerate into the absurd, the ludicrous. Was she a scholar manqué, as some have suggested? She adored research, but again, she exercised control. Research was a means to an end with her. The end being the creation of another book.

What I shall attempt, in this chapter, is to show where and how our paths actually crossed. It is a matter of regret to me that I didn't interview her when she was living at Kilmarth. But I believe firmly, having spoken to those who knew her, that the Cornish landscape had an enormous impact upon her and, therefore, her work. Her surroundings mattered desperately. That's hardly surprising, since those surroundings were perfect for her.

Think what you will about her personal life – her attitude to her father, her marriage, her close friends – she was never anything but perfectly suited to the place in which she lived. Without that stability, I very much doubt if those novels would ever have been so immensely enjoyable. For that, we can thank the Cornish landscape that she so loved.

Above all, of course, she was the supreme story-teller. A master-craftswoman in the fine art of narration.

But let us look at some of the places and the people she encountered in the 1930s.

Bodinnick-by-Fowey, as I was taught to call it as a child, had a tremendous impact upon her.

The River Fowey runs like a dream through a great work of literature, published only a year after Daphne du Maurier was born. In her nursery days and beyond, Kenneth Grahame's immortal childhood description of Fowey was recalled through the sea-grey eyes of the Adventurer, in *The Wind in the Willows*.

Daphne would have known the book from childhood and, with her imagination, have been spellbound by 'a babbling procession of the best stories in the world, sent from the heart of the earth to be told at last to the insatiable sea.'

Grahame, tragic figure as he was, was a close friend of Sir Arthur Quiller-Couch, a distinguished Cornish man of letters.

Did Daphne know of Q's injunction on writing? 'I loathe the flippant detraction of what is great,' he wrote, 'but literature is not the

DAME Daphne du Maurier, photographed at Menabilly, the Rashleigh ▶
mansion between Fowey and Par. Lying on the desk is a copy of her book
Vanishing Cornwall *which many Cornish people regard as the most*
important volume she ever wrote.

presence of any great priesthood.'

Enough to alarm, if not terrify, any would-be scribbler! But Q was too kind a man, and far too courteous to be rude to a young woman like Daphne du Maurier, with literary associations trailing like clouds of glory in her background. He actively encouraged her, sometimes, it seemed, in spite of himself. Victorian in outlook, he was not unnaturally dubious about some of the relationships portrayed by characters in the du Maurier novels with their unashamed melodrama. He would not have approved of young ladies like Daphne who perpetually wore trousers, either. But dear Q could never have imagined, surely, that this young woman – whose powers of syntax seemed non-existent – would one day complete one of his unfinished novels. As he had, in his time, completed an unfinished work of R L Stevenson.

'They'll never forgive you,' he warned her, 'for being a best-selling writer.'

But it was with Q's daughter, Foy, that Daphne was to form a long and lasting friendship. And it was in Foy's company, that she was able to explore Cornwall. Foy Q was no 'flapper'. I did manage to interview her when she was living at Lanhydrock, a National Trust property. Our merry peals of laughter rang out as she told me some of the tales of pre-war Fowey – such as being in an early motor vehicle which got out of control on Fowey's Windmill Hill and which ran backwards at an alarming speed. It was Foy's first experience of cars – and she thought at the time that it was perfectly natural they should travel backwards! Foy proved to be a great companion for Daphne.

And across the Fowey river, in an abandoned hut up the enchanting Point Creek, lived the romantic novelist, Leo Walmsley, whose book, *Love in the Sun*, an artlessly simple and sentimental love story, was an instant best-seller when it appeared in 1939. Daphne du Maurier befriended him.

These then were some of the local people whose acquaintance the would-be writer made during the 1930s. Through Foy Quiller-Couch she met Clara Vyvyan of Trelowarren, a prolific writer.

◀ *LOOKING down on Fowey from the war memorial – a photograph taken in 1948.*

Significantly, when Daphne du Maurier first saw battlemented 15th-century Trelowarren, her emotions exploded. She 'wanted to weep and hide in the walls.'

And when she, and sister Angela, first saw Menabilly, she couldn't sleep for excitement.

What, I've wondered, must she have thought as she stood, for the very first time, at Hall Walk, above Bodinnick, and high above the River Fowey, and gazed at the lovely old fishing and boatbuilding village of Polruan, immediately across the estuary from Fowey?

Often, she must have strolled through Pont – a place of solitary loveliness, when the fields beside the narrow lane in that valley were pink and white with apple and cherry blossom. Did she pick the abundant fat plums that grew wild along the riverbank – their whereabouts betrayed in springtime when the bushes flowered?

Spring there was vivacious, but autumn was blissful: rich in blackberries, elderberries, chestnuts, hazel nuts and frost-pricked black sloes – bullums, we called them, as boys.

For it was my great good fortune to spend most of the war years, and, thereby, much of my childhood in nearby Polruan.

That walk, to Pont, or further on, up hill, past the church of Lanteglos to the great sweep of cliffscape, was a very familiar one to me.

Fowey, facing east, was known as the 'sunny' side: Polruan, facing west, was the 'money' side. But Polruan was also known as 'Little Prussia'.

In such a tight-knit community, everyone knew everyone else's business. Though it was wartime, Polruan was a magnificent place in which to live. I look back, even today, and marvel still at the combination of the countryside and the sea in such close proximity. It was a totally unforgettable place.

How could a writer like Daphne du Maurier have anything but the most powerful feelings about that Fowey estuary? And it attracted her like a magnet. She was never happy, never complete, unless it enveloped her. Beyond Cornwall was a desert.

At the entrance to Pont Creek, I remember, was an old hulk of a vessel stuck in the mud. Perhaps Daphne was bold enough to venture, as we Polruan boys did, thigh-deep through that soft, warm, mud, digging for rag worms to fish with. Or endeavoured, as we

often did, to spear flat-fish stranded in the rivulets of water between the mud banks.

There were small boat yards squeezed into the narrow flat strip of land that ran back from Pont towards Polruan. The village had a wet dock called, I believe, Newquay, which was owned by the Slade family. The Slades married the Salts, and built the biggest ships. And further up river, I remember, was Brazen Island, where once a sardine factory existed. Was that fact, or the canvas of a childhood fantasy?

Ferryside itself, at Bodinnick, where Daphne du Maurier lived, had once been a boatyard, turning out one ship a year last century. Daphne could hardly fail to be deeply intrigued by it all, and, not surprisingly, she immersed herself in family history, and wove the Slades into her first novel, *The Loving Spirit* (1931). She wrote it at great speed, and was mortified when told by her agent that she would have to cut it by 20,000 words!

The following year, 1932, she married her Prince Charming early one July morning, in the venerated church of St Willow, in Lanteglos. Then they set off for a honeymoon in Frenchman's Creek.

Coincidence, coincidence: I was born in July, 1932. And I remember St Willow's best as the church in which my sister was christened in 1943. It has a nave of five bays, and a Mohun brass of 1508 on which I polished up my schoolboy Latin: 'ex infirmitate vocata Sudye' – 'she died of the sweating sickness'. Daphne's beloved Bodinnick was one of the seats of the Mohuns: All coincidence, of course.

There could be no better place for a boy than Polruan in which to live and grow. The village clings to the face of a steep hill, and, over its shoulder so to speak, are the great cliffs overlooking Lantic and Lanivet Bays.

SIR Arthur Quiller-Couch of Fowey, an eminent figure in the world of Cornish literature. A number of his novels were based on the town and he was the original editor of **The Oxford Book of English Verse.** *Dining with Q and his family at The Haven remained a crystal-clear memory for Daphne. Of such an early occasion she recalled 'It could be a bit frightening; in a way you sat on the edge of your chair. The old man could be very Victorian.'*

It was Foy Quiller-Couch who, in the 1930s, interested Daphne in helping the National Trust acquire part of this coastline. She donated some of the royalties from her new novel, *Jamaica Inn* (1936), to the Lanivet Bay Fund. She would have known that those rocky inlets that punctuate this magnificent cliffscape, were once smugglers' coves!

It was in the old Watch House, along this coastline, that Daphne used to meet Christopher Puxley, with whom she had a wartime affair. She rented the tiny stone and slate building perched over fifty feet above a cove between Polruan and Polperro. We Polruan boys probably knew that coast and its coves better than the lovers, though it was out of bounds during the wartime.

But Daphne could not have failed to observe that with no houses in sight along that deserted coastline, it was brimful of birdlife and wild flowers. Buzzards, ravens, peregrine falcons, graceful curlews with their haunting call, and the ever-present wheeling of innumerable seagulls. Did *The Birds* have its genesis here?

The cliffside fields with their velvety carpet of grass nibbled close by sheep were flecked with flowers all year round. Fat rabbits fed on the cushions of thyme in the cliff turf.

There, too, she would have seen the sea in all its moods. From the damascene serenity of calm waters, to the boiling fury of a storm. She knew that the weather was as complex as Cornwall itself.

A county where the visible surface often hides the reality. Where people, for all their curiosity about each other, are discreet, almost to the point of secrecy.

When Daphne came back to Fowey, in 1942, she lived at Readymoney Cove. The family holiday home, Ferryside, was occupied by servicemen. Her garden at Readymoney, lodge house of another Rashleigh building, called Pont Neptune, formed a part of the beach. Despite the fact that the entrance to Readymoney Cove was criss-crossed by a formidable latticework of anti-mines/submarine/landing craft posts, it was used by local schools – including my own, Fowey Grammar School – for swimming practice and events. What effect all that noise must have had on an author trying to complete her novel, *Hungry Hill* (1943), and a play, *The Years Between*, can only be imagined.

By that time, Fowey people surreptitiously pointed her out as the

RAY Bishop, the doyen of Cornwall's photographers, captures morning magic at Fowey. There is enormous variety in the water life hereabouts – and one can only guess how this activity worked on the imagination and creativity of the young Daphne du Maurier when she first came to this lovely corner of Cornwall. It was a love affair that was to last for the rest of her life.

author of *Rebecca* (it had already been filmed by Hitchcock and shown in the Troy Cinema, Fowey, to everyone's great curiosity).

My mother applied to her for a job as a housekeeper, on hearing on the local grapevine that she needed one. I was taken along as a reluctant and disinterested spectator to what passed for an interview. I wish now I been more observant. But for years afterwards, I remember my mother saying how nervous Mrs Browning was – how she had twiddled her fingers when she was talking, as if she wanted a cigarette. My mother didn't get the job: Daphne wasn't interested after she learned my mother was pregnant.

But she did need staff, as she was about to move to her beloved Menabilly, the house in which, for 17 years, she had longed to live. How she must have hated the wartime restrictions, especially the miles of barbed wire and anti-tank devices that restricted her walks along the cliffs, and down to the beaches. Perhaps, though, she approved of all road direction signs being removed during the war. Places like Polruan became almost impossible to find!

But Fowey was becoming impossibly overcrowded, and filling up with American troops. In the autumn of 1943 she turned her back on the town, and moved three miles away into her dream house. It had no water, no lighting, no telephone, no modern amenities – 'a rat ridden ruin' – but that didn't deter her.

Menabilly had been built by the wealthy Fowey merchants, the Rashleighs, in 1600, on the Gribbin headland, which juts out into the Channel. To the west, across St Austell Bay, lies Black Head and Trenarren – later to become home to one of her few Cornish friends, the great Elizabethan historian and scholar, Dr A L Rowse.

Menabilly has acquired almost folk-lore status in that people continue to believe that it is the Manderley of her novel, Rebecca. But Manderley was based primarily on her childhood recollection of Milton Hall, near Peterborough.

But she admitted that she loved Menabilly more than she loved people. Daphne du Maurier was instinctively a recluse. Menabilly's remoteness satisfied perfectly her need to be left alone.

A stone day mark, an old navigational aid, resembling a lighthouse, stands upon the Gribbin headland. It's an exhilarating place to be when there's a south-westerly blowing up-channel. Polridmouth Cove, or Pridmouth as it's known, with its freshwater lake, is tucked into the Gribbin's eastern flank. In spite of wartime restrictions on movement, Daphne and her children managed to use Pridmouth beach as if it were their very own. And her seclusion was enhanced by the V-shaped woodland: one arm running from Pridmouth Cove to Menabilly, and the other curling away through a narrow valley as far as the crossroads at which stood the legendary Tristan Stone, until it was taken down and moved into a layby, in 1970.

Here were all the visual threads that any weaver of romantic tales could ever need! And this, I believe, is the very heart of du Maurier country.

Some years after Q died, his daughter Foy invited Daphne to complete a novel about the Tristan and Iseult legend that he'd been working on. The result was *Castle Dor* (1962), and it gave her confidence to write more 'serious' works. *Vanishing Cornwall* (1967) and *Golden Lads: Antony Bacon, Francis and their Friends* (1976) followed, though she said in 1965 that once she'd written a book, she lost further interest in it.

She was fascinated by archaeology. The 6th century 'fortress' of King Mark of Cornwall, at Castle Dore, Lantyan where a mysterious, romantic love affair was played out, is merely a short distance from Menabilly. In 1936 and 1937 Dr C A Ralegh Radford excavated the site, and found King Mark's 'palace'. Not far distant, at the crossroads above Fowey, was the menhir known as the Tristan stone. 'A memorial,' said the archaeologist, 'set up above the grave of the prince in the old family cemetery alongside the road, leading to his residence, Lancien.'

The tragic love story has inspired music and verse. And for a brief

GRIBBIN Head. Time and again the sea and the coastline triggered ideas – and inspiration – for the writer.

period, their expeditions researching the Castle Dor book, brought her closer to the philandering Tommy 'Boy' Browning, her husband. Their marriage had stuttered fitfully from the time he returned home from the war.

Oddly enough, although as a journalist I never sought to interview her, I was told, in 1973, through a mutual friend, that she hoped I would continue to support the case for the restoration of the Tristan Stone to the crossroads (I was then the environment correspondent of the *Western Morning News*). It pleased me to know that she read my work as I read hers.

Daphne's last house, ironically, was to be Kilmarth – in Cornish 'The retreat of Mark.' It was about Kilmarth that she wrote the remarkably hallucinogenic *The House on the Strand* (1969). But she never wished to leave Menabilly – and she lost that house, and Tommy, within four years of each other.

Haunted men, doomed women, fallen houses, smugglers and wreckers, and the way her brilliant imagination handled them made her one of the world's best-selling authors. But she still worried about making enough money to live on! She was human, and had her weaknesses. But her strengths were greater than most. Some memories were painful. Old grievances die hard. Youth may not be renewed, Phoenix-like. No-one lives twice: once is enough.

On April 6, 1989, she was taken down, at her request, to stand on Pridmouth Beach for the last time. Three days later, she was dead. She was cremated at Glynn Valley Crematorium, near Bodmin, and the remembrance service was held at Tregaminion Chapel, close to the gates of Menabilly House, where she'd dwelt for 25 of her 81 years.

Her name will live on through her books – at least one of which some thoughtful producer, Spielberg perhaps, may, hopefully, turn into a great film; *The House on the Strand*. But for me, this slim little woman, with a warm smile, whom I can still remember, with her children in tow, walking through Fowey's sunny wartime streets, shared my own growing love – that of the Cornish countryside around Fowey. In turn, the unending riches of the place yielded themselves up to her.

And never, surely, was author and environment more exquisitely matched.

MICHAEL WILLIAMS, a Cornishman, started full-time publishing in 1975. He and his wife Sonia live in a cottage on the shoulder of a green valley just outside St Teath in North Cornwall.

In addition to publishing and writing, Michael Williams is a keen cricketer and collector of cricket books and autographs. He was the first captain of the Cornish Crusaders Cricket Club and is today President of the Crusaders. He is also a member of Cornwall and Gloucestershire County Cricket Clubs – and a Vice-President of the Cornwall Rugby Football Union. A member of the International League for the Protection of Horses and the RSPCA, he has worked hard for reform in laws relating to animal welfare.

Locally he is a patron of the Broomfield Horse Sanctuary at Trewellard.

He is a member of the Ghost Club Society, and is their representative in the south west. His latest publications include **Edge of the Unknown** investigating a wide range of paranormal cases in the Westcountry, many appearing in book form for the first time.

Outside his Bossiney activities, Michael has recently set up as a writing and publishing consultant, evaluating manuscripts and advising writers.

DAPHNE du MAURIER
– A PROFILE
by Michael Williams

THE death of Daphne du Maurier, peacefully at her home
Kilmarth, near Par, at the age of 81, marked the end of a great
literary era in Cornwall.

Novelist, short story writer, biographer and autobiographer, she
was one of the greatest authors to be identified with the
Westcountry and Cornwall in particular.

Dame Daphne came to Cornwall in the 1920s and immediately
fell in love with the place. It was a love affair which lasted for the
rest of her life.

Superficial critics saw her as a romantic novelist, but she was
more than that. She was a good psychologist, and her writing diamond sharp. She had brilliant narrative gifts and, above all, she was
a storyteller par excellence. There were often haunting echoes of
the macabre and the supernatural in her stories, and the visual
quality of her writing was so vivid and strong that it translated nat-
urally into television and cinema films.

Despite her international fame and fortune, she was a rather
reclusive person, and I was fortunate back in the 1960s when I
wrote to her asking for an interview – and she agreed. She was then
living at Menabilly, the Rashleigh mansion between Fowey and
Par.

She told me she worked to a regular pattern, writing from
10.30am to 1.30pm and from 5.30pm to 7.30pm. Occasionally she
worked for a while in the afternoon, but weather permitting, she
normally went for walks with her dogs.

Daphne du Maurier was a literary all-rounder. There were novels, short stories and sometimes long stories as in the case of *Not*

After Midnight, and biographies like the one of her father simply entitled *Gerald* which was first published in 1934. Later, much later, in 1973 she wrote *The du Mauriers*, the lives of the du Maurier family: from the departure to France in 1810 of Mary Anne Clarke, mistress of the Duke of York and the great-great-grandmother of the author to the marriage in 1863 of her grandfather George du Maurier.

In this same interview she told me about her collaboration with a dead author, the late Sir Arthur Quiller-Couch. When he died in 1944, he left behind an unfinished manuscript, and this collected dust until around 1958 when his daughter Foy decided to ask her old friend Daphne if she would complete it. She told me her immediate response had been to say 'No thanks' but on reading the half manuscript her curiosity and spirit of challenge were fired.

Both she and Foy Quiller-Couch believed the central character in the manuscript, one Doctor Carfax, was based on Sir Arthur himself.

During that Menabilly meeting which took place in 1963, she confessed '… I cannot see myself settling down to another Cornish novel.' Though *The House on the Strand* and *Rule Britannia* both lay in her writing future, *My Cousin Rachel* was her last historical novel set in Cornwall. There is a Jane Eyre atmosphere about this novel which was first published in 1951. A few years ago I saw the stage version performed at Torquay when Anita Harris played the role of Rachel. This performance underlined the author's ability to write very convincingly about women as well as men, with Rachel coming across as a mysterious woman. As for her true motives, we could argue about these for hours. Whether we read about Rachel inside the covers of this novel or see her on stage, she is an intriguing and complex character. It was a visit to Antony House in south east Cornwall around 1950 that triggered the idea for this novel. The portrait of Rachel Carew, which inspired her, still hangs in the porch room at Antony. There is, though, an important difference between the real Rachel Carew and the Rachel in the novel, in that she married Ambrose Manaton of Kilworthy and died young.

Though Daphne du Maurier lived her Cornish years entirely in and around Fowey, she had an understanding of Cornwall and the Cornish which stretched from Land's End to the western banks of the Tamar. She understood the contrast and complexity of Cornwall: King Arthur an impossibility and a probability, the Methodists and the High Anglicans, the traditional industries of mining and fishing and the modern explosion of tourism. She identified the curious division between folklore and history and, above all, she painted in words the variety of the landscape: the bleak windswept moors and the sheltered valleys and the beautiful but wicked coastline and the ever-changing seas. Here in Cornwall, the land which was the location for many of her stories, she lived simply and quietly – swimming and walking, reading and soaking up the atmosphere: all of which gave free rein to her deep inner life, her imagination and creativity.

Cornwall, in some strange way, has helped inspire and release an enormous amount of creativity. The sculptor Sven Berlin, who lived and worked for a time in St Ives, once said: 'When the sea gets into a leg I am carving what excitement there is! It goes charging through the whole of the stone, and a man, as if by magic, is transformed into an ocean with rocks and tides, shells and caves – a sea-dragon.'

I once asked about her favourite volume and received a rather surprising reply.

'Each book has given me pleasure,' she said, 'but you know, when it's completed the whole thing fades. Each has its phase.' She wrote rapidly, usually completing a book inside twelve months. Robert Louis Stevenson, the creator of *Treasure Island*, was one of her acknowledged masters, and she was passionately interested in the Brontes and their Cornish connection.

In the early days of Bossiney publishing, she was kind and encouraging – wise too in that she told me the crucial importance of two things: distribution and publicity. She also generously contributed to our first major title *My Cornwall* and, without knowing

DAPHNE du Maurier lived quietly and simply here in Cornwall – ▶ *walking her dear dogs, swimming and reading, all gave free rein to the deep inner life of her imagination. V S Pritchett said of her: 'Many a novelist would give his eyes to be able to tell a story as Miss du Maurier does, to make it move at such a pace and go with such mastery from surprise to surprise ...'*

it, we created a piece of publishing history. Angela du Maurier contributed a chapter on Fowey – the only time the two sisters appeared inside the same book.

I saw her for the last time in 1988 at Kilmarth, that lovely residence which inspired her to write *The House on the Strand*, when she kindly autographed some books for me. Incredibly the handwriting had the same strength and flourish as when I asked for her autograph more than a quarter of a century earlier. My very last sight of her was striding down the path, with her nurse some twenty paces behind her and her dog scampering ahead.

Not long before her death, Tamsin Thomas and I made a radio series for BBC Radio Cornwall on du Maurier locations west of the Tamar. As Tamsin and I moved from one setting to another, we began to understand the enormous debt the county owes to Dame Daphne. She has quite simply sold Cornwall to millions all over the world, and through her writing, places like Jamaica Inn and Frenchman's Creek – to name only two – have been immortalised.

In my library I have – I think – every book she wrote and often in reading her words I can hear that lovely voice. In her heyday she had the looks and vitality of an actress. She was, after all, the daughter of the most distinguished actor manager of his day, Sir Gerald du Maurier. She spoke with a slight but beguiling lisp, and I have, on tape, a BBC radio recording she made. The ring of her words is quite magical.

In April 1989 when she died I wrote to Esther Rowe, her faithful housekeeper and secretary and said 'Sarah Foot has asked me to write a tribute to Daphne in her magazine. It is enclosed. I did it without rewriting – and hope I have conveyed my affection and admiration of the great lady because she was quite simply that.

'When a notable person dies, it's often said that a light goes out, but not so in Daphne's case, she will live on in her writing and the films that grew out of her stories and will continue to grow out of them.'

◀ *HEADING out of Fowey for the Channel. On the extreme point is Punch's Cross where some say the boy Jesus came ashore.*

MENABILLY AND KILMARTH

by Michael Williams

W HEN you went to Menabilly in her days there, you had the definite feeling you were at the heart of her real and imaginary kingdom. One reviewer has said 'The great love of her life into which she poured her energy and dreams was a house in Cornwall: Menabilly.'

Two houses in Cornwall became more than homes for Daphne du Maurier – Menabilly and, later, Kilmarth, were spiritual havens.

Both properties, owned by the famous Rashleigh family, exercised enormous influence in her life and in her writing. But before either there had been Ferryside at Bodinnick which had been purchased by her father Sir Gerald. This later became the home of her sister Angela and for the young Daphne it had been a magical introduction to Cornwall: coal fires on winter evenings and then in contrast watching the gulls and the kingfishers in summer and always the magic of Fowey harbour. Angela du Maurier, writing about Ferryside in the 1970s, reflected: 'to live in Fowey by the water's edge as I do is a constant source of interest … War years I remember thinking the thing I would care most to see would be the twinkling lights of the harbour once again.'

Menabilly stands some three miles from the harbour and when as a trespasser with her sister Angela, searching for the large empty house, she thought 'perhaps it is a house of secrets and has no wish to be disturbed.' But on her next visit to Cornwall she rose at 5am and resumed her search for the elusive Menabilly. In *The Rebecca Notebook* she recalled: 'I edged my way onto the lawn and there she stood.' Windows shuttered, ivy covering grey walls, the house, like most of Cornwall, was sleeping at this hour.

MENABILLY, seat of the Rashleighs, depicted in a hand-coloured engraving of 1822.

Daphne never forgot that abortive first visit when the over-grown drive made it all seemingly impossible and it was that experience which fired her to write that memorable opening line: 'Last night I dreamt I went to Manderley.' Little did she realise that this beautiful Cornish mansion was to be her home for more than a quarter of a century. *Rebecca*, one of the bestsellers in the world of publishing, achieved fame in five art forms: a novel, a play, a film, an opera and a television series. The setting for the novel, first published by Victor Gollancz in 1938, is largely shaped around the grounds of this property, and Manderley is significantly based on Menabilly.

This, her most famous novel of all, was written in the first person, with an odd twist. Not once in all these pages is our heroine given a name: not she herself, her husband or her servants, who call her Mrs de Winter. In an interview with Janet Watts in *The Observer* in May 1981 she said: 'One's whole life has been pretending – a sort of acting. I think it's an inherited thing. People said "Gerald du Maurier acts himself ..." but no he didn't ... when acting, he was pretending to be someone else and in writing you're pretending to be someone else, especially when you write in the first person. You become that person.'

Elsewhere Daphne du Maurier has touched on the process of writing: 'The child destined to be a writer is vulnerable to every wind that blows ... The essence of his nature is to escape the atmosphere about him, no matter how stable, even loving ...'

If Ferryside captured her heart, then Menabilly captured her whole being. This was deeper than a woman falling in love with a view. Now she was spellbound by Cornwall's atmosphere and haunting history. Now hand in hand with Cornwall, her writing career was accelerating. Why did she write? She made no bones about her motivation. 'My main object was financial independence.'

Alfred Hitchcock's *The Birds* is a classic film, and although he changed it, the original story really took place here in this corner of Cornwall. It was based on the farm Menabilly Barton with the farmer ploughing and her going for an afternoon walk and seeing those gulls circling round the farmer's head. In an extraordinary moment she suddenly though 'What if those birds attacked?' In this single episode on a Cornish farm we learn something about her as a person – her character, her range of interests and her inner vision. All of which reminds us that she came from a creative family. Her grandfather George du Maurier became a celebrated figure through his drawings in *Punch* and her father Gerald was more than a matinee idol, he was a great innovative actor.

On the subject of du Maurier creativity, we must not forget younger sister Jeanne who lives at Manaton on Dartmoor: a gifted painter. She paints still life, flowers and landscapes. Jeanne's palette is high keyed. The fact is she cares more for colour than form. Then there is the older sister Angela, another writer. I

remember when *My Cornwall* appeared, Daphne told me how well Angela's chapter read. 'I wish Angela would write more like that,' she said. But then Angela's autobiography was tellingly entitled *It's Only the Sister*. There is also the photography of son Christian Browning whose brilliant pictures lit so many pages of *Vanishing Cornwall*. Henry Trevor, reviewing the book in the *Cornish Review*, said '... Mr Browning is a photographer of great sensitivity, and it would indeed be difficult to find much fault with the photographs in this book – they are sometimes a little over-dramatic, perhaps, but then so is Cornwall, and by and large they capture the mood admirably.'

In the same review Henry Trevor referred to the author's concern for preserving: 'Cornwall – that is, the Cornwall of romance and mystery, of strangeness and the unknown – is slowly vanishing. One day, if things continue at the same pace, it will be gone altogether, and it will be too late then to complain ... Miss du Maurier is to be commended for drawing attention to many trends and facts which, perhaps, we tend to forget ... there can be no doubt she cares deeply about what is happening and in these days to care is half, no *all* the battle.'

Daphne's love affair with Menabilly was limited by the turning of the calendar and a lease. She described leaving Menabilly after 26 very happy years as 'the most appalling wrench.' It was a painful twist in her life that her husband, who liked the look and atmosphere of Kilmarth died a few weeks after the signing of the lease – and never lived there. A one-time dower house to Menabilly it is little more than four furlongs away and has splendid views out to sea. She soon made Kilmarth *her* home: memorabilia occupying the walls and window sills, furniture, books, portraits objects, gilded

◄ *MENABILLY: an old photograph. This splendid old house belonging to a distinguished Cornish family was largely the Manderley in Daphne du Maurier's* **Rebecca***. Susan Hill writing in the* **Sunday Times** *offered this thoughtful assessment: 'The novel is as unforgettable as its opening sentence. When people talk of Rebecca they remember where they were when they first read it ...' Today it is the home of Sir Richard Rashleigh: a private residence, it is not open to the public. Daphne du Maurier lived and wrote here for more than a quarter of a century.*

china and photographs of the Royal Family, as well as her own.

This grand old house, overlooking the majestic sweep of the bay beyond, began to spur Daphne's curiosity and imagination and the result was *The House on the Strand*, first published in 1969. Part straight novel and part suspense story, this is a spell-binder and how and why it has never been turned into a film must remain a mystery. Dick Young has been lent a house in Cornwall by a professor of bio-physics. He agrees to act as a guinea-pig for a new drug which the professor has discovered. The bottles containing the drug, are waiting for him in the laboratory at Kilmarth. Dick Young takes the prescribed dose and finds himself back in Cornwall in the fourteenth century. He takes various 'trips' into this past and finds himself on the edge of intrigue, adultery and murder. Are the experiences hallucinations? Are they a subconscious escape from his own marital life? Or has he genuinely trav-

KILMARTH near Par, Daphne du Maurier's last Cornish home. She lived here from 1969 until her death in 1989. Today the house is much changed – this photograph was taken during her time at Kilmarth. It is private property and, like Menabilly, is not open to the public. Kilmarth in ancient Cornish means 'Retreat of Mark.'

elled back in time? These 'trips' become an addiction and come to final and dramatic climax.

The House on the Strand is a fascinating mixture of the here and now and Cornwall in the fourteenth century. Such is Dame Daphne's research into earlier centuries in many of her books that we, the reader, feel we are on some kind of time machine. For example I happen to think *The King's General* tells us more about life during the civil war in Cornwall than many history books. Likewise *Jamaica Inn* evokes the very spirit of Bodmin moor in the old days. But equally she could encourage us to look forward as in *Rule Britannia*, and herein lies some of the du Maurier genius.

1993 saw a new dimension to the du Maurier story: the publication of the sequel to *Rebecca*: Susan Hill's *Mrs de Winter*. As Daphne du Maurier had carried on the Q story all those years ago, now Susan Hill moved *Rebecca* into the future – with one important difference. This author faced a special challenge. Many of us who had read and enjoyed *Rebecca* had questions and thoughts of our own. Is Maxim in the clear? Will Manderley be restored to its former glory or another kind of glory? Is he still a rich man? Some people even believed no sequel should be written, arguing they usually disappoint and somehow interfere with the imagination of the readers. But *Mrs de Winter*, published by Sinclair-Stevenson, is a triumph for both author and publisher, successfully reviving old du Maurier characters like Mrs Danvers and Jack Favell, inventing new ones and bringing it all to an eerie Cornish conclusion. Kate Saunders, reviewing the book in the *Sunday Times*, said: 'Hill has the gift of running up an intense, doomy atmosphere out of no more than a crow's call and a wreath of Cornish mist. And she writes at least as well as du Maurier. Best of all, she brings a keen intelligence to the task, understanding both the dynamics of the original and the special elements that have enthralled so many readers.'

DAPHNE du Maurier first discovered Bodmin Moor while riding a horse, and more than half a century on it remains the best way of exploring the landscape. These riders are in the area of the Trippet Stones on Manor Moor.

REBECCA PICKFORD has been working as a journalist in Cornwall for nine years, seven of those years as a reporter, producer and presenter for BBC Radio Cornwall, during which time hers became one of the best – and best known voices on Westcountry radio. She is married to a solicitor, and with their two children they live in beautiful countryside near Truro.

Born in Somerset, Rebecca Pickford gained an Honours Degree in English at University College, Cardiff. Her communications grounding was in newspapers and she moved into broadcasting in her early twenties. Today she writes short stories and features for magazines like **Woman &** **Home** *and* **Homes & Gardens**. *This is her debut for Bossiney.*

BODMIN MOOR
by Rebecca Pickford

THE search for artistic inspiration can be long and hard. We've all heard of great authors being forced to lock themselves away in silence to combat writer's block, or musicians chasing that elusive sound, and artists returning again and again to the same painting to find that missing something. We've also heard of Cornwall's famous tradition of art. With its sweeping sands, foreboding coastline, winding lanes and quaint harbours, it is easy to understand that this is no historical quirk. But there is one place for me that does more than just inspire. Stand on Bodmin Moor and take a few deeply exhilarating breaths of the air and I guarantee it will unlock something inside you.

Just say the words to yourself now – 'Bodmin Moor, Bodmin Moor, Bodmin Moor', and others will follow. Craggy, coarse, legendary, dark, tempestuous, romantic, windswept, rugged, isolated, raging. There are more – illusory, mysterious, primitive, timeless, beautiful. It is as if the very thought of it is enough to liberate even the most pre-occupied.

There can be few people who remain untouched by this landscape. It even gets to me when I'm encapsulated in a speeding car en route to Truro and beyond. If it wasn't for the moor's preference for mist and drizzle (or 'mizzle' as we call it) I would insist on you winding down your window next time you are passing through and testing its power for yourself! Of course, the only way really to feel the moor's magic is to get out there, whatever the weather, and take those deep breaths. Lean against its rocks, run your hands in its streams, feel the gorse, touch the heathers, and let the wind rip right through all those twentieth century cares. Bodmin Moor is sure to evoke something in you, but one thing is for sure – it will not be a cosy feeling of Mother Nature nurturing her flock.

It certainly did something for Daphne du Maurier, quite apart from providing her with the perfect setting for perhaps the most famous Cornish novel ever written. Her haunting tale *Jamaica Inn* opens with a wet and wild coach journey across the moor. She writes of a lashing and pitiless rain, stinging the windows of the coach. She uses words like 'hard', 'barren' and 'bare'. The trees are 'bent and twisted from centuries of storm', and her heroine, Mary Yellan is already filled with a dark fear of the place. Having come from the lush, green calm of the Helford river, some forty miles west of Bodmin Moor, Mary is overwhelmed by the harsh edge to nature. She thinks how 'there would never be a gentle season here' and even summer would be extreme, turning the grass to yellow-brown before May had even begun.

So, Bodmin Moor is barren, pitiless, fearful. Certainly, Mary Yellan fears it. But it is also intriguing, romantic and wildly attractive. Its persuasive lure is very hard to resist and once you have succumbed, prepare to be forever under its spell!

Like many, my first acquaintance with the moor was from a car – a battered old Mini that kept me in transit throughout my student days. Like Mary, I had an unsettling introduction to it, because, in the tradition of the best horror movie, I broke down at Bolventor, a stone's throw from the famous inn itself. Of course, it had to be getting dark, and the rain had to be lashing the windscreen as I got out of the car and wondered what on earth to do next. This is where the similarity with horror ends, because, within minutes, I was in someone's kitchen, drinking coffee and phoning my father to come and get me! This is also where I part company with Mary Yellan and her opinions. During her arrival journey, as the wind and rain batter against the coach, she muses that even the people on the road and in the villages 'changed in harmony with their background.' I found, much to my permanent gratitude, that the Cornish hospitality is alive and kicking in the moorland communities.

You simply cannot live, or stay longer than a fortnight in Cornwall, without seeking out this place. It was a matter of months before I was back on Bodmin Moor, this time on the highest hill in

THE former Rectory at Altarnun, now Penhallow Manor, a delightful country house hotel. A Georgian style house, constructed in 1842, it stands alongside the village church, dedicated to Saint Nonna, and known as a key location in **Jamaica Inn**, *the home of the albino Rev Francis Davey, the arch-villain of the story. The eighth and ninth chapters, in the eye of her imagination, are set in the living room as Mary Yellan sat and watched the smouldering turf fire – and discovered the grim truth behind her uncle's smuggling. The woman, who has been seen walking from the church to the old rectory, is believed to be the ghost of Mrs Tripp, the housekeeper of a one-time vicar.*

Cornwall, Brown Willy, being blown to pieces by the most glorious summer wind I have ever experienced. It was one of the sort of days that Cornwall does best – balmy inland, breezy on the coast, and with a relentlessly sunny and blue sky. We decided, en masse, to make the rough and stony mile-long walk to the foot of Brown Willy before climbing the 1377 feet to the top. I wore fairly sensible shoes and a summer dress, and we picked a slow, lazy, chatty way to begin our ascent. We must have been in decadent mood, because the one bag we carried was full of smoked salmon and champagne. Our purpose was to toast as much of Cornwall as we could see once we arrived at the top.

I remember thinking how Daphne du Maurier might have tempered that sentence 'there would never be a gentle season here' if she had been with us then. But that was before we reached our pinnacle.

As my dress flapped so furiously in what seemed like gale force gusts and stung my bare legs with the sheer speed of movement, as my cries of wonder and surprise were swept away and reduced to nothing, as the view went on for ever and ever, never touching upon dual carriageway or town, I too thought there would never be a gentle season here.

I have since been back again and again, and both I and the moor have been in many different moods.

Dozmary Pool has just about as many moods as you can conjure up. Sir John Betjeman is quoted as saying it has 'a brooding melancholy, especially at evening' and certainly, as I approached it, silently and stealthily one autumnal evening, it began to work a spell on me. I had been in a chatty, lively mood, and it had been my idea to visit Dozmary. We had both heard the Cornish ghost story of Jan Tregeagle and how his wicked spirit was supposed to have been banished to the pool and forced to empty it with a leaking limpet shell – payment for his murderous and evil life. He is said to have killed his first wife and children to marry an heiress, who also died by his hand – an act that he repeated rather too often in life, until he ended up selling his soul to the devil when he died. The story goes that, a few days after his death, Tregeagle was summoned to Bodmin court to stand witness in a debt trial. The debtor, believing that Tregeagle was well and truly dead, denied the charge, only to be haunted at a later date by the malevolent Jan! The debtor, terrified by the evil spectre, called in an exorcist vicar. Dozmary Pool seemed to be the ideal place for such an unpleasant character, especially as the story also insists that the lake is bottomless!

We also knew it was associated with the legend of King Arthur – could this really be Excalibur's home, the pool into which Sir

39

*CONTRASTING faces of Bodmin Moor: the Cheesewring and a windshaped tree on the eastern side of the moor and, right, King Arthur's Hall on the other side with Rough Tor and Brown Willy in the distance. Daphne du Maurier loved and understood the subtleties of this landscape, and her novel **Jamaica Inn** captured the very heart and soul of Bodmin Moor.*

Once known as Fowey Moor, it has a wealth of Cornish history and folklore, and sometimes it is difficult to know where history ends and legend begins. Often one feels compelled to ask 'Can there be smoke without fire?' It stirs our curiosity and invites speculation.

Bedevere threw the bejewelled sword on strict instructions from the dying king?

And, much as I love fiction, I also thought I would be left largely untouched by it – I simply wasn't in the right frame of mind to be moved by atmosphere … or so I thought!

The surface was completely still. I wanted to disturb it, just to check that what I was seeing wasn't an illusion, but I knew I couldn't, or daren't. There was a dankness to the air, almost cave-like, and yet here we were, in one of the most barren spots of Cornwall. And I had to fight a desire to enter it. Did it really beckon me? I know I will return to find out, and in the meantime, I have made it my business to find out more.

The pool is a mile in circumference and it lies about 900 feet above sea level. Deer used to drink at it, and there lies the answer to another of its little mysteries. Many an amateur archaeologist has uncovered the weapon used by Stone Age man to kill these creatures. Tiny pieces of flint, inserted into a stick have been picked up in and around the scrubland of Dozmary – a seemingly pathetic tool with which to pierce what is a graceful but hefty beast, but history tells us that they did the trick.

And then, of course, there is Jamaica Inn – or, in Daphne du Maurier's words, Bodmin Moor's 'one grim landmark'. She writes how it stood alone in glory, foursquare to the wind, just as it does today. And later, when Mary Yellan explores the inn more thoroughly on her first morning, she discovers 'unexpected rooms', again, just as you can today. Mary describes a heavy atmosphere, reminding her of the last time the room was full, a taste of old tobacco, a smell of sour drink, and the image of warm, dirty bodies sitting too close to each other on the dark wooden benches.

Jamaica Inn still stands alone in glory, foursquare to the wind, and it is still packed during opening hours with humanity, although today's customer is a little more discerning so the old tobacco and sour drink smells are long gone. What is there, however, is an unexpected room, and one well worth a second glance. Look for the Daphne du Maurier room, and there you will find her study desk and her trusty typewriter, bought by the present owners to create a mini museum to the woman who made their home known the world over.

When Daphne du Maurier wrote *Jamaica Inn*, in 1935, it was a temperance house and perfectly hospitable stop-off point on the twisting journey from Bodmin to Launceston. She and her friend, Foy Quiller-Couch, stayed there in the early thirties and Daphne asked Foy to join her on a horse-riding trip to explore the moor. They set out on a bright sunny morning, but failing to recognise the change in the weather, they soon found themselves in an all-enveloping fog. They tried for hours to find their way out of the heavy mist, but everywhere looked the same and they eventually had to accept that they were completely lost. After much panic, the moorland horses started to lead the two women out of their trouble and on to familiar paths. The experience was an immediate inspiration for Dame Daphne, and although she can not have guessed at its significance, the seed of her novel started to grow. She read *Treasure Island* during the same stay, and somehow, the three places – the moor, Jamaica Inn and Robert Louis Stevenson's fantasy isle – merged. The ideas of wrecking and smuggling seemed to fit with

THIS photograph of Jamaica Inn, taken from an old picture postcard, is probably fifty years old. ▶

THE FAMOUS JAMAICA INN

which stands right in the heart of Bodmin Moor, Cornwall, on the old coach road from Launceston to Bodmin, which is now part of the main A 30 road LONDON to PENZANCE. The cobbled court remains and on crossing this and opening the great wooden door, one beholds a veritable museum of relics from the past, muskets, swords, brassware, etc., with a timbered ceiling, and a great log fire, and a stone-flagged floor. A mile away is Dozmary Pool and the moor is packed with associations of Daphne du Maurier's famous novel.

An old picture postcard.

43

the grey slate inn, with its tall chimneys, 'forbidding and uninhabited'. A literary classic was born.

It was published in 1936, and was a huge success. The film rights were soon sold, and so the Jamaica Inn we think we know was born. I think it is part of the moor's mystery that the real story behind Jamaica Inn remains largely untold. It is also great testament to Dame Daphne's name that the image it enjoys today is purely down to her imagination and skill as a story teller.

Much of Bodmin Moor's mystery and trickery is timeless. It has undoubtedly been playing such pranks on its human visitors for centuries. But never let it be said that it doesn't add to its repertoire as the years roll by. A walk on Rough Tor (pronounced Row Tor) on another still, fine day proved this to me.

THE Daphne du Maurier Room at Jamaica Inn. It is only right and proper that the inn at Bolventor, immortalised by Daphne du Maruier's novel of the same name, should honour her with some of the memorabilia from her last home, Kilmarth near Par.

It is the second highest hill in Cornwall, Brown Willy's little brother, and equally as beautiful. Cattle still graze the slopes below, its crags cut an intense outline if the sky is blue. This time, I was well prepared in jeans and tee-shirt for the wind to lash me to bits. Surely this pleasant climb would offer no real surprises. My reward would be, at 1296 feet, the view. This time, I thought, I would appreciate the summit in an entirely different way. Well, I was right about that, but how dare I presume to assume?

As I stood again on my majestic moorland balcony, taking huge gulps of the whistling wind and marvelling at the expanse, a deafening noise grabbed me and shook me off my pedestal. The noise got even louder, angrier, screaming. For a split second, I was in total confusion. What was happening? Was the world about to end? Then a monstrous and terrifyingly close low-flying fighter plane screeched overhead. I saw its ugly metal under-carriage and I could even pick out the numbers and letters on its body. I felt complete outrage, but my anger was on behalf of the placid moorland cattle we had passed on our way up. When I stopped shaking, I started laughing. Bodmin Moor had done it to me again!

I might have been shaking before I even set out if I had already been told of Bodmin Moor's most convincing ghost story. It belongs specifically to Rough Tor and concerns a young cripple called Matthew Weeks, and his eighteen-year-old sweetheart Charlotte Dymond. They both worked at an isolated farmhouse known as Penhale, and would walk together across the moors on their days off. Charlotte, however, was a flirt and a tease, and she would tell her jealous crippled boyfriend of imaginary sweethearts. On Sunday April 4 1844 she must have over-stepped the mark. They both set out for a walk, but neither of them returned. Her body, with throat cut from ear to ear, was discovered in an old stream near Roughtor Ford. Her murder aroused so much anger that a special railway line was set up from the moor to Bodmin Prison where 20,000 people watched the hanging of Matthew Weeks. The date was August 1844.

A monument to Charlotte Dymond still stands on the marshes below Rough Tor today and there are many stories to be told of a young female ghost seen roaming the moors.

Perhaps, with all its dark, brooding, satanic eeriness, you could ask why there aren't many more tall stories of ghostly visions on the moor. It is, after all, a vast and unknown territory. It can easily claim lives without any help from man at all. Exposure to its fierce elements might be enough to bring a weak, or inexperienced, explorer down. But the moor has all the answers, and there is a good one to this question. Why gild the lily?

If you need to read, or to be told, text book narrative of predictable supernatural tales, if you want the hairs on the back of your neck to stand, momentarily, on edge, or if you want to feel that shiver down your spine as you make your way to bed, then open a good book, or go and see a Hitchcock movie.

If, however, you want to experience something entirely first hand, if you want the atmosphere to be wholly of your making and not conjured up by special effects or clever words, if you want the landscape to speak to you and only you, then you know where to go. At the risk of repeating myself, I guarantee that a few moments on Bodmin Moor will unlock something inside you. Cornwall is giving you the key.

THE most famous inn sign in all Cornwall – some might even argue in all Britain. Throughout the year thousands and thousands of visitors are photographed standing beneath this vivid and, at night, illuminated sign. Jamaica has had a varied past – both temperance house and posting house in the 1800s. It was Sir Arthur Quiller-Couch who suggested to Daphne that she and his daughter Foy should make a horseback expedition of Bodmin Moor and stay at the then temperance house – and the two young women did just that in November 1930.

FELICITY YOUNG lives at Tintagel with her husband Ian, daughter Hazel, horse Red and dog Digger. She is a painter, book illustrator and author. Since 1984 she has contributed more than 350 illustrations for a whole range of Bossiney titles.

Felicity Young is the co-author of **King Arthur in the West,** *and in 1993 she made two radio broadcasts on Arthur and his links with the Westcountry. She did an earlier broadcast on the craft of illustrating books.*

In 1989 she made her debut as a Bossiney author, contributing a chapter on Lawrence of Arabia in **Dorset Mysteries.** *Then in 1990 came her first book* **Curiosities of Exmoor.** *In 1991 she wrote about Charlotte Bryant, a small-time prostitute in* **Strange Dorset Stories** *and the following year she explored 'Strange Places', a chapter in* **Strange Stories of Cornwall.**

Felicity is also the co-author of **Tintagel Reflections** *which contains many of her own illustrations especially done for this publication.*

THE KING'S GENERAL
by Felicity Young

CORNWALL is often referred to as du Maurier country. If you read any of her novels you can immediately see why. She writes with such feeling for her beloved Cornwall, the storyline of each one enhanced by her detailed description of Cornish people and places. *The King's General*, her fifth novel written unusually quickly in three months, is full of such detail about her particular piece of Cornwall. Menabilly where she lived, the narrow neck of land between Fowey and Par and other historic sites, Castle Dor, Launceston Castle and Pendennis Castle are all brought to life by her pen. She blends fact with fiction to create a story woven around seventeenth-century romance and civil war, a delight to any lover of Cornwall who cannot fail to feel in tune with Daphne du Maurier's own passion for the county. Famous places and well-known Cornish families are put into historical context as a backdrop to a romantic tale of a General and his love. It is a sad but very readable story, factual and enlightening. The effects of the civil war upon Cornwall and its people are seen through the eyes of a woman crippled by a riding accident, her whole world changed dramatically; sadness, bitterness, unrequited love and the unfairness of the war and her personal situation are the ingredients. The scene is set at Menabilly and the cast is the family and household playing out a drama which contains elements of truth blended in du Maurier's unique style of fictional writing.

In *The King's General* Daphne du Maurier describes Launceston Castle where Sir Richard Grenville was imprisoned before being exiled in Holland. This Norman structure dominates the town of Launceston, often called the 'Gateway to Cornwall'. It was a site

chosen wisely as from the summit of the mound on which it was built there is a commanding view of the landscape from Bodmin Moor to Dartmoor, the wild landscape stretches for miles, an ideal vantage point from which to watch for the enemy or to control a strategic position in time of war.

Pendennis Castle at the mouth of the river Fal is also featured in the book. It is a well-known fortress best remembered in history for the longest siege during the civil war. Daphne du Maurier shows her knowledge and insight into Cornish history when she mentions the battle at Castle Dor where Parliamentary forces under the Earl of Essex fought a hard fight to no avail. She has brought her home, Menabilly, in the parish of Tywardreath, to life giving her personal impression of how life must have been there in the seventeenth century. Tywardreath is steeped in history and Menabilly, the home of the Rashleighs, a well-known Cornish family, stands within its boundaries. The parish churchyard holds many secrets and some of the tales must have fired the imagination of Daphne du Maurier. She touched on so many places in Cornwall and even allowed her story to stretch out into Devon. Plymouth, Tavistock and Exeter are all put into the context of the civil war. Families such as the Grenvilles, Arundells, Trelawneys, Sir Arthur Basset of Tehidy, and the list of famous Cornish names goes on (though sometimes the spelling is slightly different) – all given their due within the pages of the book. This personal touch gives her story a certain credence for the avid 'Cornish' reader; there is plenty to recognise and enjoy.

◀ *LAUNCESTON Castle keep and grounds photographed by the Cornish Bard Joan Rendell MBE in 1981. The pump once stood inside the prison wall. Launceston Castle is featured in* **The King's General.** *Times were when it was a notorious place and the expression 'as bad as Launceston Jail' summed up the feelings of local people.*

Also pictured is Doomesdale, a small dank room in the north gate of Launceston Castle. Doomesdale got its name because of the belief that prisoners cast in there seldom came out alive.

The King's General by virtue of its romantic yet tragic tale would make a good film. It has been sadly overlooked. It remains one of Daphne du Maurier's lesser known books, compared with *Jamaica Inn* or *Rebecca*. All du Maurier's skill and sensitivity shows through each page: 'a fascinating cobweb of romance and drama …'

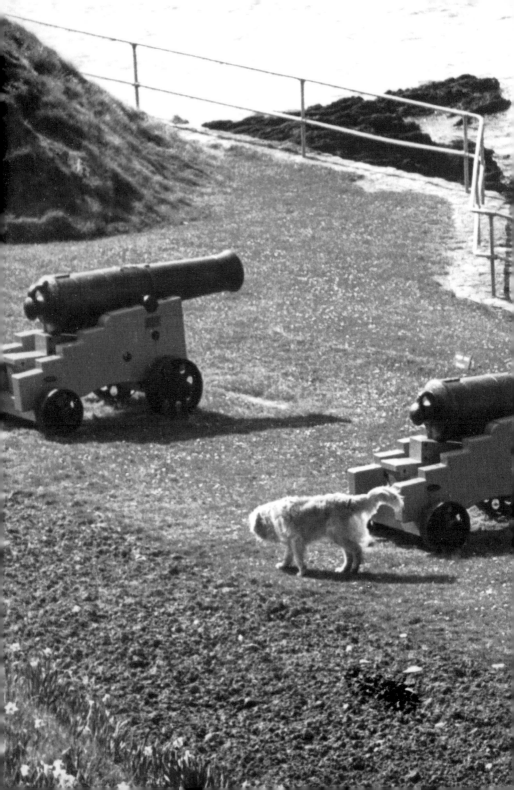

*PENDENNIS Castle overlooking the River Falmouth was the scene of one of the longest sieges during the Civil War, another Cornish fortress featured in **The King's General**.*

SARAH FOOT lives in a beautiful converted barn at Elmgate, overlooking the River Lynher, and she has strong family links with Cornwall. Her grandfather Isaac Foot was Lord Mayor of Plymouth, and her father Hugh Caradon was born in the city. She lived for some years by the Tamar, and knows and loves both western and eastern banks of the great river.

Before becoming involved with full time social work, first at Derriford Hospital and now at St Luke's Hospice in Plymouth, Sarah Foot was a prolific contributor to the Bossiney list. She made several television appearances and many radio broadcasts.

*In 1994 Sarah Foot introduced **Secret Devon**, in which six writers made six journeys. More recently she was co-author of **Magical Places**, a journey in words and pictures from Land's End to Lorna Doone Country. Her earlier titles **The Barbican** and **The River Tamar** remain in print.*

FRENCHMAN'S CREEK
by Sarah Foot

DAPHNE du Maurier's genius for understanding the essence of Cornwall, is in my view, unique. No other 'foreigner' or person not born or bred in Cornwall has had the imagination or the perception to be able to, firstly, appreciate the atmosphere of Cornish places including moorland, river valleys, and coastal reaches, as she did, and then to transcribe these feelings into powerful novels. It did not take long for Dame Daphne to become an honorary Cornishwoman' accepted for her love of the place and its people by all the Cornish.

Frenchman's Creek is just one of the more secret parts of Cornwall that she discovered, promptly falling under its spell and proceeding to use it to such great advantage as a background for her book of the same name.

I have made several visits to Frenchman's Creek in different seasons of the year. Each time it has moved me but in very different ways. The first time was in the spring when primroses carpeted the banks and pathways and the trees were in bud. There was a stillness and a hush about the place that kept my friends and myself from needing or wanting any conversation. The few people that we passed smiled in wordless welcome, it would have felt a crime to break that gentle silence. This is a tidal inlet of the great and beautiful Helford River and on my first visit the tide was in, moss covered trees lay collapsed into the water, the birds sang brightly, every now and then the persistent call of a cuckoo rang out across the water. I felt then, that as we sat on the bank and drank in the tranquil atmosphere of trees and water and spring flowers, there was a door that shut this place off from the rest of the world and

TWO aspects of Frenchman's Creek down on the beautiful Helford River. It is a mysterious magical place but you will find it on any worthwhile map of Cornwall hard by the village of Helford. **Frenchman's Creek**, *published in 1941, prompted Daphne du Maurier to make this interesting comment: '... this is the closest I have come to writing a romantic novel ...'*

The creek has a genuinely haunted reputation. Peter Underwood, Life President of the Ghost Club Society, in his **Westcountry Hauntings**, *published by Bossiney in 1986, wrote:*

'In days gone by the Creek is said to have been fordable at certain points, on certain tides, even where its mouth now joins the Helford River. One night, so runs the story, an old man took the short cut across the Creek. Unfortunately he had been drinking, and perhaps he had the tide wrong, but at any rate he did not return home that night.

'In the morning he was found, for the tide had then receded, sitting upright in the water, with his hat still on his head, his long white beard running with water. Ever since, early on certain but unspecified mornings, when there is an unusually low tide, the same figure has been seen where the old man met his death and also, somewhat mysteriously, his ghost has suddenly appeared in neighbouring cottages and houses that he knew during his life.'

that nothing could ever change it.

Later, driving home I remembered that Lady Vyvyan had once written about her first visit to the Creek and had expressed the same sort of feeling. Lady Vyvyan had lived at Trelowarren House nearby and was a Cornish writer of pure genius. She had loved the Helford River and probably knew its surrounding banks and woods and fields better than any other human being. She was a great walker and thought nothing of walking alone for miles in the surrounding countryside often on moonlight nights. She was able to convey the atmosphere most brilliantly in her books.

When I looked for her description of Frenchman's Creek in her book *The Helford River* I was not disappointed. She wrote this passage before the Second World War. 'The first time I rowed up to the end, or rather the beginning, of the Creek was on a day in September. I remember looking up through the trees and seeing a glint of gold from the fields where the corn stood in shocks and as I

LADY BROWNING, as she was by her marriage to General Browning, beside her beloved boat. She and her husband, after their wedding at Lanteglos Church, headed in their boat for Frenchman's Creek.

rowed on and on, the line of water narrowed and the trees behind closed in on me, keeping me safe in a place where no trouble could enter, where the ancient gods were surely reigning in serenity.'

But although her feelings of peace and tranquillity corresponded so well with those which I felt on my first visit there is most definitely another side to Frenchman's Creek – more often referred to as The Pill by local people.

As far as Daphne du Maurier was concerned this was a mysterious place, a place of almost eerie atmosphere. In the first chapter of *Frenchman's Creek* she writes: 'The solitary yachtsman who leaves his yacht in the open roadstead of Helford, and goes exploring up river in his dinghy on a night in midsummer, when the nightjars call, hesitates when he comes upon the mouth of the creek, for there is something of mystery about it even now, something of enchantment ... he pauses resting on his paddles, aware suddenly of the deep silence of the creek, of its narrow twisting channel, and he feels for no reason known to him that he is an interloper, a trespasser in time ... and as he creeps forward the creek narrows, the trees crowd yet more thickly to the water's edge, and he feels a spell upon him, fascinating, strange, a thing of queer excitement not fully understood.'

I had forgotten this passage from Dame Daphne's book when I first went up the creek by boat, but it still surprises me how the atmosphere from the water differs from that of the river banks. I felt then, as the boat slowly crept up the creek, a heavy melancholy about the place. The drooping branches of trees touched the water, the tide was in, the quiet of the place was ominous, almost frightening. It was a relief when we made our way out into the wider reaches of the water. I would not have liked to trespass on those waters on my own – it was intriguing but not at all comfortable. So very different from that earlier spring visit I had made many months before.

No wonder Daphne du Maurier chose this secluded mooring and meeting place for the lovers in her book *Frenchman's Creek*. To Dona and the Frenchman this was a secret place where they could hide from the rest of the world and for a time live their lives in a carefree romantic way. Only someone who truly understood this inlet of the Helford river could have written so movingly about it.

To learn more intimately about the Helford River and Frenchman's Creek I once went and spent a week with a friend who had taken a cottage at Helford – it was an idyllic time. Just being in the little hamlet was a completely new experience. The little cottages huddle around the river and if you sit with the windows open on a summer's evening people's voices drift through the soft night air, gentle and comforting without seeming to be intrusive in any way. Strangely the sounds of that riverside reminded me of Dylan Thomas's '**Under Milk Wood**'.

Sadly, most of the cottages are now owned by outsiders, part-timers, and no longer by people indigenous to the area, but yet the atmosphere of timelessness remains. Things may have changed dramatically along the banks of the Helford River but somehow despite the new buildings, the smart new motor vessels and the loss of an indigenous population and their tasks, the mixture of peace and gentleness with another stranger presence of something beyond our ken will always remain. It is this contrast that is the creek's great feature, a place to love and yet a place that holds you at arm's length never truly giving away its secrets.

◀ *ANGELA du Maurier, Daphne's sister, on the left, showing author Sarah Foot the garden and view at Ferryside in 1979, when Sarah was researching her book on the River Fowey. Earlier Angela du Maurier had contributed a chapter in* **My Cornwall:** *the only occasion when the two sisters appeared inside the covers of the same book. In the page alongside this photograph Sarah Foot wrote: 'Over the years the du Maurier family have modernised the house but left all its old magic. The back wall of the house is still the rock of the cliff behind and it is built on three storeys so that one feels as if one is on a boat, especially on the second floor where all the rooms lead off a long narrow passage like cabins.'*

ST CATHERINE'S Castle at Fowey which was built by Henry VIII during his wars with France. In 1786 a chart, drawn by Lieutenant James Cook, cousin of the famous explorer, showed the seaward defences of Fowey. This castle houses six cannon and even the blockhouses, then approximately four centuries old, supported a five-gun battery. There is an excellent account of St Catherine's in action inside the pages of **Frenchman's Creek.**

JANE TALBOT-SMITH was born at St Veep, the third daughter of Tim and Ruth Lumley-Smith – so she has known du Maurier Country from her earliest days.

In 1957 the family moved to St Breward where her mother ran a very successful children's hotel. After school at Camelford, Jane left Cornwall for college, work and travel.

Following two and a half years building horse-drawn vehicles, she decided leather was the medium for her, and took up a place at Cordwainers College, Hackney, London. Later Jane worked under Master Saddler Les Coker, famous for his sidesaddle used regularly by the Queen. In 1980 she and her husband Michael returned to Cornwall to set up her Blisland Harness Makers in the lovely Fowey Valley below Jamaica Inn. In 1985 she was assessed and accepted into the Society of Master Saddlers and became the first Master Saddler in Cornwall. Jane rides and drives her own home-bred horses and regularly competes in Driving Trials with the Great Western Harness Club. This is Jane Talbot-Smith's debut for Bossiney.

RULE BRITANNIA
– the FINAL NOVEL
by Jane Talbot Smith

ONE can well imagine Daphne du Maurier sitting at her desk and then gazing out over St Austell Bay, the wind blowing on-shore rattling the window frames and dislodging slates and won-dering what would happen if foreign troops were to land on the beach below; this indeed is the theme of *Rule Britannia*, her thir-teenth and last novel.

Emma, a lovely girl of 21, is living in Cornwall with Mad, child-ish shortening of Madam, her now retired but distinguished grand-mother, and Mad's six adopted boys of various ages from 19 to 3, in the house, Trevenal, up on the cliff above Poldrea. Waking one morning in early November Emma is trying to decide what to do, to leave or not to leave Mad. The radio isn't working, on going downstairs they find the telephones cut, the post hasn't arrived, there is a continual drone from waves of planes overhead and an army of soldiers is crossing the field towards the house. The neigh-bour's farm dog, Spry, is shot. This small incident starts off the chain of events for the whole book.

This is fictitious time in the future when the UK has been with-drawn from the Common Market and, with the threat of bankrupt-cy, it has been decided by the coalition government that the solu-tion lies in a union with the United States, to become USUK. Writing in 1971/72, Daphne du Maurier forsees not only Princess Anne becoming Princess Royal and Prince Andrew the Duke of York, but the use of obscure languages for passing messages. Cornish is spoken alongside Welsh on the short-wave radio, as today the US marines use Navaho Indian speakers. She also sees how Cornwall, with high unemployment and little or no industry,

A MEMBER of the Castle staff is taken in stately progress by a local boatman to St Michael's Mount.

is to be turned into a theme park for tourists, so aptly put by the Poldrea fishmonger Tom Bates: 'Turning us into a fairground, with all this talk about going back to the old days. Before we know where we are they'll have us all dressed up as smugglers and pirates and the like.'

Theoretically USUK is to be an equal partnership; but to some people it soon begins to look like a takeover bid. It is through her love of the Cornish countryside that one feels Daphne du Maurier understands that Cornwall has a great sense of difference from the rest of England and I'm sure she identifies with Mad when she says: 'I was born in Wimbledon ... but I've made this corner of this particular peninsula my home for a long time now, and I'd certainly die for it', and it is this feeling which she uses to justify Mad's determination to resist this domination by the US forces and put into operation a series of events to defend her beloved Cornwall, gleefully abetted by the boys and many of the neighbouring farmers and friends. These events soon paralyse this microcosm of England and 'what fun it all is,' for Mad is a truly theatrical character who sees everything from the stage, much to the concern of Emma.

The book is dedicated to Gladys Cooper, a long-time friend of the whole du Maurier family. I remember as a child of five when my godfather the actor Alan Napier, who will be remembered for his portrayal of Alfred – Batman's butler, Mongo to the family, came to stay and we were all invited to visit Angela and Jeanne du Maurier at the family home of Ferryside in Fowey. The talk was all of this theatrical world and way above my head. For me what was memorable was not the famous people, but the natural rock wall of the sitting room. It even had water running down it!

The shoreline and the tides of Cornwall play their part in the book too. Terry, fleeing the marines after a fight escapes by running along the shallows and scrambling up Little Hell and hiding there in a gulley in the cliff-face. But on leaving he slips and crashes about twenty feet to the cliff bottom breaking his leg in the fall. He was lucky to be found by the beachcomber before the tide came in and drowned him. Later the beachcomber uses the cliff and tides to dispose of an unwanted body.

When things start to turn nasty for the marines they come in

JANE Talbot-Smith, on the right, and Cornish broadcaster Tamsin Thomas of Fowey riding on Bodmin Moor. Here they pause on the rim of Dozmary Pool. According to ancient legend the dying King Arthur ordered that his sword Excalibur be thrown into Dozmary.

heavy handedly and take away for questioning all the men and older boys. We hear they have been taken to the Scilly Isles, but in fact it is Lanhydrock. The marines, admitting defeat, withdraw to St Mawgan to take off.

This, her last novel, is Daphne du Maurier at the height of her writing – perceptive and drawing lifelike characters and with a real sense of Cornwall and the Cornish. It shows the effect of what is virtually an occupation, on local people and the relationships between them. Who is willing to collaborate, and who are Mad's allies, prepared to go to what lengths to disrupt this 'union'? In her persona of Mad I feel that Daphne du Maurier is identifying with the real Cornish people and, as such, the Cornish people take her to their hearts.

◄ *PAR Beach on a September morning. Though there are no real place names in the novel* **Rule Britannia**, *there are mentions of St Michael's Mount, Falmouth and St Mawgan, but readers who know their Cornwall, will understand the location is St Austell Bay and Par Beach. Dame Daphne's last wholly historical novel set in Cornwall was* **My Cousin Rachel** *published back in 1951 – a story with a Jane Eyre quality of suspense and tragedy.*

DOUGLAS WILLIAMS has been a journalist in West Cornwall for more than forty years. He was born in Newlyn and lives in the fishing town today. Married with two daughters and two grandchildren, he is deeply involved in the life and work of the district through various music societies, Rotary Club, Methodist Church and Newlyn Harbour Commissioners.

He has contributed five titles to the Bossiney list, the latest being **About Penzance**. *Douglas Williams is a Bard of the Cornish Gorsedd, and his Bardic name sums up his interests: 'Voice and Pen'. His* **West Cornwall Camera** *also remains in print, in which he provides the text for many photographs of the late Harry Penhaul.*

REDISCOVERING 'VANISHING CORNWALL'

by Douglas Williams

WHENEVER people of the 'born and bred and proud of it' variety talk to me about Cornwall for the Cornish, I am inclined to switch off. After all, my ancestors have only lived in Newlyn for four, five or is it six generations or more. On both sides of the family!

I know of the immense contributions made by those who have come here to live, whether in retirement, for peace of mind, to hide, or all three.

That jocular poet and satirist, Arthur Caddick, had the merry answer when it was claimed that one needed to be Cornish to reflect the true Celtic spirit in art. 'O Auntie, fetch the family tree, have I Cornish blood in me?' was his riposte.

Rowena Cade, creator of the Minack open-air theatre, Dorothy Yglesias and sister 'Pog' of the Mousehole bird hospital and sanctuary, have surely earned a place alongside Dolly Pentreath, Mary Kelynack and the other celebrated ladies of our Duchy.

Why, we have had our first non-Cornish-born Grand Bard of the Gorsedd in George Ansell – a notable leader – and have our first woman as non-Cornish-bred Lord Lieutenant, Lady Mary Holborow.

I have been to art exhibitions of paintings of Cornwall where not one of the ten artists had this mystical birthright halo.

Have then, the much-maligned 'foreigners' taken over? Not quite, but their work for the cultural life and environment of Cornwall should never be under-estimated. While re-reading *Vanishing Cornwall* by that supreme story-teller, Daphne du Maurier, I became more aware of their influence, and of hers.

It was back in July 1967 that it was first published – I remember going to a book launch – with the new edition in 1981 illustrated by the photographs, most in colour, by son Christian Browning. That of the rain-dashed window looking out over gardens close to the Fowey estuary, is my favourite study.

The outpouring of affection in *Vanishing Cornwall* is emotion recollected in humility and with unique insight. Her vivid yet precise prose style, with its full flowing good sense and sensitivity, never orotund, make it a loving and lustrous testament.

She knew the county from Launceston to Land's End, its coves and cliffs, the heroes and traditions, its ancient places and history. Modestly she wrote of how she 'rambled on about the past' but the readers knew how she found content in this island kingdom.

'The beauty and the mystery beckon still,' she wrote. As they always did, from the age of five. Menabilly and du Maurier will always be linked with such classic novels as *Frenchman's Creek*, *Jamaica Inn*, *My Cousin Rachel*, and *Rebecca* … 'Last night I dreamt I went to Manderley again.'

The author did more for tourism than many a slick holiday promotion or advertising campaign. She conveyed the true magic of Cornwall, made millions weep, laugh, and be richly moved by the quality of her writing, its euphony, and the realities she portrayed.

We all seek beauty, adventure, fantasy, the chimera of victory.

Her messages and her fears remain diamond sharp and clear. 'The spirit of the local people here about does not change!' she wrote, but realised the changes going on in industry, in fishing and in agriculture.

Granite quarries have closed, quotas and even more regulations dictate the work patterns on land and at sea. The fishermen and farmers have lived with the wild winters, working on through the storms, but a bureaucratic flood is something new.

A march through London's streets was not enough to save Geevor tin mine at Pendeen. The last mine in Penwith is a heritage centre. South Crofty remains the sole, and last, tin mine in Cornwall.

◀ *THE RASHLEIGH Inn at Polkerris. Some of the cottages hereabouts were built by the enormously unpopular Preventive Service. The Cornish did not approve of anything or anyone who discouraged smuggling …*

Those 'last hunters', the fishermen strive to hold on to their fishing grounds and their livelihoods. Will they and their children have to find new industries and homes thousands of miles away, as so many had to do in the 19th-century?

'You Can't do Less
Than drink Success
To Copper, Fish and Tin!'

Unemployment remains unacceptably high, wage levels low and modern house prices way above the ambitions of many who want to stay and bring up their families in their home county.

The dual carriageways roll on, the approaches to major towns often blighted by a forest of signs and a sea of roundabouts. Out-of-town stores add to the pressure on the business life of the traditional centres.

The number of cars on our roads has possibly doubled or trebled since *Vanishing Cornwall* was born. There is hardly a little street without its row on row of parked cars by day and night.

Daphne du Maurier understood the spirit of Cornwall and the Cornish: she was also one with them because she respected their religion and heritage, their legends, even their folklore and superstitions.

Did Arthur stride this land, did the young Jesus come with the trader Joseph of Arimathea? Did Jack the Giant Killer slay Cormoran upon St Michael's Mount?

Cornwall has been the home of the finest of British artists. Turner came, Munnings stayed for a while, Lawrence lived near Zennor, Russell at Porthcurno and Dylan Thomas was wed at Penzance.

Betjeman was at his most serene at St Enodoc, Hepworth and Leach created their finest sculpture and pottery at St Ives. Rowse, Causley and Tangye still sing of the glory of Cornwall.

The creative skill and the craftsman's art are as cherished as ever. The magnificent Tate Gallery, St Ives, has proved both a popular success and of immense benefit to the town. In one parish there have been major developments by the Royal Geological Society of Cornwall, the Penlee museum and gallery and the Newlyn Art Gallery, celebrating its centenary.

Now, more than ever, planners are zealous in 'fending off'

schemes to infiltrate the beauty of our coastal environment.

The National Trust is ever faithful. As more and more of the coastline comes under their stewardship so comes more security for the future.

The new challenge is whether Cornwall will become a conservation corner of England, a museum, a playground, one huge retirement home?

The important qualities endure. The view of ocean from a headland, the feel of the damp 'mizzle' on an autumn night, the ever-present sounds of the sea, the sight of the day dying in the west in the majesty of summer. These cannot be effaced.

The lifeboatmen continue to serve with courage and glory, the male voice choirs sing their hearts out, the young rugby players dream of wearing the 'Black and Gold.'

'The Merry Morning of May' is still echoed with passion at Padstow. The Helston bandsmen keep that melody for the Furry Day dance of grace and formality ...' The band with the curious tone of cornet, clarinet and big trombone.'

The silver ball is still thrown and chased at St Columb and St Ives:

'Town and Country do Your Best For in this parish I must Rest.'

The beacons blaze on Midsummer Eve, the Gorsedd ceremonies bring their colour to the first Saturday in September. To vanish is to disappear.

The corn is still in the shock and the fish are still on the rock. We do not want to live on memories and there will be changes – as there have always been.

It is how we rise to the challenges that will prove if we are worthy to walk in the footsteps of our forefathers.

'By Tre, Pol and Pen, Ye shall know the Cornish Men.'

Daphne du Maurier wrote: 'Treasure still lies beneath the Cornish soil awaiting harvest ... particles unfelt, unseen, coursing through the blood, directing impulse. The challenge is to the young.'

THE ELEGANCE and style of the Furry Dance shine from this old Helston
photograph. Flora Day remains one of the great days in the Cornish calendar.

79

◀ *LOOKING upriver from the Fowey Hotel.*

*Back in 1976 I asked a team of authors – as on this 1995 occasion – to contribute a chapter apiece for a Bossiney title called **Eccentrics of the West**, and Dame Daphne kindly wrote the introduction. Alas, it was a rare case of a Bossiney project not getting off the ground. So here, seeing the light of publication day nearly twenty years after it was written, is her chapter.*

MW

ECCENTRICS
by Daphne du Maurier

HOW do we define eccentricity? The *Concise Oxford Dictionary*, my only aid, gives various meanings to the word. 'Not having its axis, etc, placed centrally . . . moving in an irregular orbit,' is one of these, and to my way of thinking rather pleasing. The reader has an instant vision of a body, or bodies, shifting its path in the world, or hemisphere, according to personal whim, influenced by nothing and by no one. This surely is a more interesting rendering than 'an odd, whimsical person.'

The twelve characters we shall come to know in the following pages are not by any means all whimsical, but they certainly moved in an irregular orbit. Odd, perhaps, in that they thought and acted in an original way unlike their fellows, but so does a genius, a mad-man, and a prophet, and these are not necessarily eccentric. If the truth be told, each of us either hides, or flaunts, some little sign of eccentricity. The first, impelled by some inner compulsion to walk always on the lines of a pavement rather than the squares, or to col-lect old discarded tubes of tooth-paste until they fill a chest-of-drawers, conceals his passion from the world; the second, yearning for attention and so to boost morale, will strip himself naked in a public place and risk arrest rather than be ignored.

Flattered at being asked to write this introduction to *Eccentrics*, let me admit my own small singularity, which may be shared by others who are fortunate enough to live in rural surroundings. I do not talk to my plants, as some do, but I converse with sheep and cattle in their own language. They understand me. My baa accent is impeccable with the sheep. The ewes look up, and answer. I enquire after their health, and that of their lambs, and they reply.

SHEEP in a field above Par Beach.

My accent is not quite so good with the cattle. They stare for a moment or two before uttering their mooing acknowledgement. But rapport has been established. They resume grazing. I pass through them, commenting on the weather, whether warm or cold, and am on my way. We are friends.

I like to think, when a lamb bleats after me, or a calf stares, that its mother says to it 'Tis only the old girl from up the hill. She'll not harm you.'

So, having made my point, let us to the business in hand and to our twelve eccentrics.

As the only woman amongst the assembly, Nancy Astor is given pride of place and opens the series. Was she truly an eccentric though? The reader must judge for himself. Original, lively, frequently exasperating to her fellow MPs, even those who were her friends, she won the hearts of the people of her Plymouth constituency, by dancing light-heartedly on the Hoe between air-raids, thus inspiring them with courage to do likewise.

Perhaps it took an American to light the spark in the slower-moving British, their travel in orbit being more regular – and as an American too she knew the value of publicity. One of her best quips was a retort to a heckler at Plymouth who shouted out 'How many toes has a pig got?' and quick as a flash came the answer 'Take off your boot and count'. A great character, but not whimsical.

Sabine Baring-Gould, Frederick William Densham, and John Hugh Smyth-Pigott were all three Ministers of the Church, and as such must be treated as an ensemble. Curious, surely, that three out of twelve eccentrics should have been men 'of the cloth', and one is led to the conclusion that there must be something fundamental in the pastoral calling that turns so many incumbents to – shall I say, bizarre behaviour?

Baring-Gold was the least endearing of the trio, to my view, possibly not to others, and is remembered chiefly today for his hymn *Onward, Christian Soldiers* which has never lost popularity. He was a man of many talents, and was a novelist as well as a hymn-writer, and combined the two offices of parson and squire in his home parish of Lew Trenchard in Devon, where he succeeded his uncle as incumbent at the age of forty-seven. It is hard to assess from his life-story whether he was truly a man-of-God at heart, or like many others of his generation, as sons of nineteenth-century landed gentry, automatically chose the Church as profession. His pastoral work took second place besides his wider interests, travelling, designing, folk music, etc. His marriage to a humble mill-girl when he was a young vicar, lately curate, caused much raising of eyebrows at the time, and this again suggests a taste for the unusual; one whose horizon was not limited to the narrow circle of his own station in the world.

I must admit having greater sympathy for the Rev Densham, Rector of Warleggan, not only because I personally braved his snarling Alsatians and waved to him over his high-fenced garden hedge, but because, having now learnt much more about him from the account that follows, I believe that much of his eccentricity developed through the lack of Christian sympathy amongst his parishioners. Had they made the slightest effort to understand him he might have responded, and he certainly would not have died untended and alone, a sad recluse. No effort seems to have been made to contact either his brother, or his solicitor after his death, to discover anything of his former life and habits, and whether he had always been 'irregular in orbit', strange in his ways, or simply a lonely man lacking a single friend.

The Rev Smyth-Pigott possessed not only friends, a wife, a mistress, and a community of devotees, but had the unmistakable advantage over both the Rev Densham and the Rev Baring-Gould by believing himself to be the Risen Lord. Blasphemous, no doubt, a scandal, an outrage to the world beyond his private sect of Agapemonites, but comforting to his own ego and to the band of faithful followers at Spaxton, Somerset. After all, did it matter so much if a minister of the church should identify with his Creator and Saviour?

As a novelist and biographer I dare to sympathize, for there is no obsession like that of living night and day with a character either conjured from the imagination or from reality, and for a priest whose whole life-style must be based upon his Maker the merging of fact and fiction would have double strength. As with the Rector of Warleggan, stories spread through village, town, and indeed county and beyond, as to what rites went on behind the walls of the Abode of Love. Black magic, vice, unspeakable orgies, things too shocking to be mentioned.

The 'Messiah' departed this life in 1927, his 'spiritual' wife became head of the community, and it was not until after she died in 1956 that the so-called unholy chapel was open to the public and press.

And I quote: 'Shrouded in black against the west wall stood the altar, furnished with a cross and two highly polished candlesticks. The tall white candles were lighted as mourners arrived ... Above the altar hung two large pastoral scenes in oil, painted by members of the community. On one side was The Madonna and Child; on the other, a large framed photograph of the Ark of the Covenant church.

This does not sound like Black Magic. May the self-styled Messiah, the Rev Baring-Gould, the Rev Densham, and all eccentric ministers rest in peace.

The Risen Lord of the Abode of Love might have had a fellow feeling for Herbert W Haydon had they met. They could at least have discussed the life above in all its eternity, for Haydon, scientist and inventor, declared that he travelled to Venus by space-ship every year, and sometimes stayed there for as long as six weeks. He was, indeed, he said, ambassador on earth to the very advanced and splendid people the Venusians, who were incidently vegetarian by principle. There was little Haydon did not know about regular and irregular orbits – Venus stood still from April to May. It was unfortunate for this delightful enthusiast for space travel that he died alone in his attic before man landed on the moon or probes were sent to his favourite planet, yet on second thoughts perhaps it was just as well. His world would have indeed disintegrated had he learnt the truth that Venus was pure carbon dioxide without life.

How he would have enjoyed though the company of another of our team, the famous cricketer W G Grace, for one of Haydon's inventions was a super cricket-bat. Indeed he insisted that his greatest achievement had been to teach the Venusians cricket.

WARLEGGAN Church on Bodmin Moor. It was here that the Rev Densham lived and conducted his eccentric ministry which Daphne du Maurier wrote about in **Vanishing Cornwall**.

W G, that most likable personality who scored so many centuries for Gloucestershire and the MCC playing his last match when he was sixty-six, may not score so high in the eccentricity stakes, but his maternal grandfather George Pocock certainly qualifies.

He, like Haydon, was an inventor, and his carriage Charvolant, powered by a couple of high-flying kites, could be seen any day during the early part of the nineteenth century bearing himself and his family to Bristol and the surrounding countryside. They went at a spanking pace, and on a voyage to London passed the affronted Duke of Cumberland in Hyde Park, who, in carriage-and-pair, progressed at a more leisurely pace. What a pity that we have no kite-drawn vehicle today! How splendid if the internal combustion engine had never been invented, and instead of a thousand cars roaring down our motor-ways each one of them flew a soaring kite, like an individual standard, to become perhaps hopelessly tangled and thus put an end to all further progress.

One single individual of our merry bunch of inventors survives in 1976, and upon him I pin all my hopes of transport when crisis

comes and petrol stations are closed to motorists throughout the country. Harold Bates, who lives near Dartmouth, has run his own car for ten years not on petrol but on chicken manure, and informs his friends that his device can be fitted to any petrol-driven engine that exists. No ingenuity needed. Merely a supply of chickens to ensure the droppings that form the gas. So, I wonder if it must be chickens, or whether my friends, the neighbouring sheep, might oblige? I must get in touch with Harold Bates and find out before the fatal moment strikes.

Richard Cockle Lucas and Alfred Wallis were the only members of our group with artistic talent. Cockle Lucas, a nineteenth century sculptor, and Wallis a rag-and-bone merchant who became a professional painter at the age of seventy. To the layman's eye, he was the more endearing character of the two. Fisherman, rag-and-bone dealer, plus ice-cream seller, plying between Penzance and St Ives,

POLRIDMOUTH Bay: the beach house and the lake. Dampe Daphne used this area for important scenes in her hugely successful novel Rebecca.

it was not until three years after his wife's death, in the year 1925 that he observed to a friend: 'I don't know how to pass away my time. I think I'll do a bit of painting'. Nor did he refer to his cottage in St Ives, but to original work, from memory or from life, on canvas. Primitive work maybe, but professional enough to win praise from Ben Nicholson, Barbara Hepworth and many others. Fame never spoilt him, and when he was dying in Madron Workhouse in 1942, all he was concerned about was that the money he had earned from his paintings should go to seamen's orphans in Plymouth.

Cockle Lucas had a higher opinion of himself, and his works, for it pleased him to write his own epitaph at the age of fifty, although he was to live a further thirty-three years, and highly flattering to the sculptor it was too.

'He Felt The Beauty Of Truth and Boldly Expressed It ... His Intellect Was Enquiring, Acute & Penetrating' are among some of his personal virtues he extolled, and if he is remembered today rather more in Southampton, where he lived and worked, than elsewhere in the world, proof that he made an impression after his death lies in the fact that a wax bust of a girl, which had been sold for a few shillings when he died, was thought to be a hitherto unknown work of Leonardo da Vinci and exhibited as such in Berlin in 1909. Cockle Lucas would have accepted such an honour as no more than his due.

Thomas Pitt, second Lord Camelford, and William Beckford, were contemporaries, near enough, though Beckford was fifteen year the senior, and both were members of the landed gentry, Pitt indeed of the aristocracy. Both inherited fortunes and estates. Both had a passion for travel. Here though all resemblance ends.

Thomas Pitt may have led a sheltered childhood in the family home Boconnoc, Cornwall, but a desire for a sea-faring life drew him into the Navy, and for more than ten years he endured every sort of danger, deprivation, even degradation – when flogged three times for criticising his superior officers – yet none of this broke his courage nor his pride, nor, unfortunately for him, his too-easily aroused temper, which finally closed his Naval career. His own end was typical of the man. He died in agony, aged only twenty-nine, after fighting a duel.

TYWARDREATH Church 1995. This parish, more than any other throughout Cornwall, influenced the author in her imagination, research and writing.

William Beckford, good-looking, talented, intellectual, with homosexual tendencies, would have found himself more at home in our present twentieth century than in that of the nineteenth. Indeed, he would have been a popular figure in society today, and unlikely to be labelled an eccentric. Gossip and scandal would not have banished him abroad, and when he did return, far from being shunned by his neighbours, the Gothic building he designed for himself in Wiltshire might well have become the showplace of the county, with Beckford showing his accumulated treasures to visitors, instead of retreating behind his walls, an embittered recluse.

Not so interesting to read about, maybe, but had he been accepted by society, as he knew it, Beckford, like the Rev Densham a hundred years later, might have lived a happier man.

So there we have them, our twelve eccentrics, and the reader may find some enjoyment by placing them, in fantasy, round a dinner-table, and imagining the conversation. Nancy Astor would, I venture to think, speak longest and loudest, but if Herbert Haydon sat upon her right he might well smother the many bon mots of the Member for Plymouth Sutton with a description of a cricket match on the planet Venus. One thing is certain. He might remain silent throughout the meal, but at the conclusion of the repast the Rev Smyth-Pigott, the self-styled Messiah and Risen Lord, would take precedence over his clerical brethren and say Grace. Even Nancy Astor would have no riposte.

I wish you entertaining reading, and take my leave. I have a pressing engagement with a ewe who wishes to consult me on the upbringing of two foster-lambs.

TREGAMINION Church which stands between Menabilly and Kilmarth. It was here that Dame Daphne's funeral service, a very private ceremony, took place.

POSTSCRIPT

It has been a special privilege to publish this, Bossiney's 232nd title. I like to think Daphne would have been pleased to see that we have reached such a publishing score.

These pages, the words and photographs, are a vivid reminder of how Cornwall, with its mystery and strange qualities, helped to fashion her international reputation. Denys Val Baker in his very good book *The Timeless Land* posed the interesting question whether Daphne du Maurier would have achieved such fame had she lived in Tooting or Surbiton. I have no doubt: it would have been a different kind of fame.

We Cornish, may not like to admit it but murder and mystery appeal to many of us and therefore novels like *Jamaica Inn* and *My Cousin Rachel* strike a chord. But Daphne du Maurier was not all Cornwall and not all novels. We must not forget her short stories. In many of them she keeps us turning the pages and makes our flesh creep.

Then there are her works of non-fiction. In addition to *Vanishing Cornwall*, she wrote *The Infernal World of Branwell Bronte, Gerald, The du Mauriers*, and *The Golden Lads* and *The Winding Stair*, volumes about the lives and times of Sir Francis Bacon, Anthony Bacon, the Earl of Essex and their colleagues. Though she will always be best remembered as a novelist – a weaver of spells – she was equally at home with the craft of biography.

In the end and in the context of this publication we must come back to a point west of the Tamar. Denys Val Baker once referred to Cornwall as du Maurier Land. That is true, but our *Cornish World of Daphne du Maurier* reminds us of something else: her Cornwall lives on in our imagination and will live on in the hearts and minds of readers not yet born.

Finally, a small but recent experience: I climbed to the top of Rough Tor early one September morning – only the animals and the birds – the spirit of *Jamaica Inn* all around me. In one of her novels Daphne du Maurier refers to the dead coming back to look at the living. Surely though she will never die or fade away.

October 1995   **Michael Williams, St Teath, Bodmin**

More Bossiney Books ...

SECRET CORNWALL
Introduced by the well-known Cornish broadcaster Madeleine Gould, seven writers make seven journeys.

'... *highlights some real secrets* ...'　　　　　**North Cornwall Advertiser**

SECRET DEVON
Introduced by Sarah Foot who in her thoughtful opening chapter reflects:

'... *scattered over the country is a strong primordial something ... that makes Devon a secret land.*'

WEST CORNWALL CAMERA
Photographs by Harry Penhaul
Text by Douglas Williams

100 YEARS OF THE EVENING HERALD
by James Mildren
'... *some century and some news!*'

MAGICAL PLACES
by Sarah Foot and Michael Williams
A tour from the Lizard to Lorna Doone Country. This is Bossiney's 230th title: 'an important milestone' says the publisher.

MYSTERIES OF SOUTH WEST
by Tamsin Thomas of BBC Radio Cornwall.
A tour of ancient sites in Cornwall and on Dartmoor.
'*There is little doubt that Tamsin Thomas has become the 'Voice of Cornwall.'* '
　　　　　Ronnie Hoyle, North Cornwall Advertiser

DISCOVERING BODMIN MOOR
by E V Thompson

BODMIN MOOR THROUGH THE YEARS
by E V Thompson

STRANGE TALES OF THE SOUTH WEST
by Ronnie Hoyle

THE MAGIC OF DARTMOOR
by David Mudd
'... *a valuable addition to Dartmoor literature.*'
　　　　　June Glover, South Hams Group of Newspapers

PSYCHIC PHENOMENA of the WEST
by Michael Williams
The subject of a Daphne Skinnard interview on BBC Radio Cornwall.

EAST CORNWALL IN THE OLD DAYS
by Joy Wilson
'... a rich choice of early Cornish photographs ... Joy Wilson provides an interesting starting point for the reader wanting to enjoy a journey into the past.'
The Cornish Guardian

KING ARTHUR IN THE WEST
by Felicity Young & Michael Williams

CORNWALL – LAND OF LEGEND
by Joy Wilson
An exploration in words and pictures of legendary sites.

KING ARTHUR COUNTRY IN CORNWALL
by Brenda Duxbury, Michael Williams and Colin Wilson

CURIOSITIES OF EXMOOR
by Felicity Young
'... a tour in words and pictures of the National Park embracing Somerset and Devon.'
Nancy Hammonds, Evening Herald
'Felicity Young, an artist who has contributed many drawings to Bossiney Books, makes her debut as an author with a beautiful description of Exmoor and its many delights.'
June Glover, South Hams Group of Newspapers

We shall be pleased to send you our catalogue giving full details of our growing list of titles and forthcoming publications. If you have difficulty in obtaining our titles, write direct to Bossiney Books, Land's End, St Teath, Bodmin, Cornwall.

Back Cover:
DAPHNE du Maurier on the steps at Kilmarth